Let's Fly

GREGORY GRANT

Ordering Information:

Prime Seven Media
518 Landmann St.
Tomah City, WI 54660

Printed in the United States of America

I AM

I AM a boy who is very proud of himself even though he is a bit disabled.
I WONDER if people talk behind my back.
I HEAR people being kind to their friends.
I SEE people trusting and talking care of their friends.
I AM a boy who likes what he hears and sees.
I PRETEND that I am a guardian angel who has been
sent down here to guide and protect everyone.
I FEEL happy when people are happy.
I TOUCH people when they are hurting.
I WORRY about everything that is going on.
I CRY when people are cruel.
I UNDERSTAND people when they are hurting.
I SAY people are kind when they want to be.
I DREAM that I am in a place far away from the fighting.
I TRY to make everyone reason with everybody.

I AM a boy who is feeling proud of himself.

This poem is to make people realize disabled people are normal people too and are not to be taken for granted.

BE KIND! WE HAVE FEELINGS TOO.

Written by Greg Grant
©1994

THE LONER

There is a boy who is a loner.

He rides the streets everyday.

People stare at him everywhere he goes but he doesn't care.

What ever he does gives him satisfaction.

There is no such word as can't.

He will prove it.

If people say he can't

HE WILL DO IT!

Written by Greg Grant

©2003

THE ROAD THAT NEVER END

There's a long windy road that they call the road that never ends.

Everyone travels on it in his or her lifetime.

It is very hilly.

Up and Down.

But it is a must.

The journey is very powerful.

You must learn from it.

If you don't you will suffer from it.

So be good and do what it says.

Written by Greg Grant

©2003

PEOPLE

Some people are big.

Some people and small.

People of all races unite.

We must all rise above and be heard.

For if we don't.

No one will hear.

People just think they know.

So, let's us be heard and known.

Written by Greg Grant

©2003

POOL

There is a pool with clear water, but it is a cesspool.

Every time you go in it.

You're not sure where you are going.

You feel like you're drowning in it.

Everywhere you turn people are staring at you.

You know you must get out.

But you can't

Written by Greg Grant

©2003

MAN'S BEST FRIEND

There is a dog.

His name is Jake.

What a lovely dog he is.

Walks alongside his master's bike.

Everywhere he goes people stop and pat him.

What a nice friendly dog.

He won't bark or bite.

Just cries if he is left out in the cold.

When he comes in, he is very happy

Written by Greg Grant

©2003

DISABILITY

There are many disabilities.

Some are good.

Some are bad.

But everyone is equal.

No on should judge on appearances.

If they do, they won't get to know people for what they are.

If you see a disabled person walking by.

Just say 'HI'.

Written by Greg Grant

©2003

AGE

Age is just a number.

Just because you are a fraction older.

They think you're too old for them.

But they don't realize there is a wealth of knowledge.

So, they are missing out on what you know.

They think it is 'COOL' to hang out with their own age.

But it is even 'COOLER' to hang out with older people.

You should try it sometime.

Written by Greg Grant

©2003

BEDTIME

Bedtime isn't for me.

It is lonely time.

But a peaceful time.

Where you can rest from a long day.

It gives you time to think.

But don't think too hard or you won't sleep.

Some time it is hard to get to sleep.

With the thoughts running away with you.

But don't fret they will calm down soon.

Close your eyes for tomorrow is another day.

Written by Greg Grant

©2003

LIFE

Life is a challenge.

Life changes everyday.

You must change with it.

For if you don't someone will make you change.

It is difficult to change.

But it is all about growing up.

But change for the good not the bad.

Change to help people.

Change to better yourself.

So, start changing today.

Written by Greg Grant

©2003

GRUDGES

Grudges come when you least expect them.

They can come in form of jealousy.

You can see people with grudges everywhere you go.

Grudges are not good.

People do have them big people and small.

You find grudges hard to let go.

When you do, you'll be at ease with yourself.

So, try your hardest to let go.

You'll be better off.

And they shouldn't come back.

Written by Greg Grant
©2003

SPIRIT OF CHRISTMASS

Christmas is a joyous time.

It is for forgiving.

It is a time for sharing.

It is also a time for families.

You don't want to be sour.

Or the day is worthless.

And out of the blue someone will be nice to you.

So be happy not grumpy.

It will make a difference for you and your friends.

Have a great Christmas.

Written by Greg Grant

©2003

FANTASY WORLD

We all live in a fantasy world in some form.

All of us pretend that nothing could happen to us.

But one day the fantasy becomes reality.

And then we must face it head on.

It is better to not think about fantasies.

Because your fantasy could be the downfall of you.

So, it is better to live a real life instead of a fake one.

Written by Greg Grant

©2003

STAR

There is a big bright star in the sky.

It is a wondering star.

When you see it, it will lead to places near and far.

It will make your dreams come true.

This star looks over you to make sure you're being good.

And if you're good it will shower you with glory and sunshine.

But if you are bad it will rain on you.

It will even help you through the bad times.

So, every night looks up in the sky and you will see it.

Written by Greg Grant

©2003

FRIENDS

Everybody needs friends to make the day go faster.

They are always there when you need them.

Sometimes they are not there.

When you don't have a friend, it hurts.

To find the right friend for you, takes years.

But one day someone will come by and will be your friend.

Until that day comes don't be scared.

Written by Greg Grant

©2003

TRIERS

There are triers everywhere.

Trying to do their best.

It you try hard enough you will be respected for it.

But if you do you must try at work or play.

If you try you will be considered one of the best.

Trying is fun.

Trying to succeed, you will get rewarded.

Written by Greg Grant

©2003

LABELS

Labels are names, some are good, and others are bad.

But you take no notice of them.

It you do you will become a label just like the rest of us.

So, if someone labels you take no notice.

Because they are just labels.

They mean nothing.

If you worry about them, you will get nowhere.

So just keep working regardless.

Written by Greg Grant

©2003

HOT DAYS

Hot days are good for sunbathing.

Hot day are good for going to the beach.

Hot days are for drying washing.

Better be careful you don't burn.

For sunburn can bring skin cancer.

It may be fun while it lasts.

But when you get cancer it isn't fun.

Written by Greg Grant

©2003

BOWLING

Bowling is fun.

Bowling is great.

It's for every one of all ages.

You go there to play.

If you take the game too serious you will lose the game.

If you go, there to have fun you will be surprised.

Written by Greg Grant

©2003

MYSTERIOUS MAN

I am a Mystery to everyone.

No one knows what the to think next.

I can do many unique things.

Many people don't know what I will do next.

Which is the mystery of it.

But the problem of being a mystery man is people misunderstand.

Written by Greg Grant

©2003

ACCEPTANCE

Acceptance is a funny word.

It means to accept one regardless of the abilities of the person.

But that is not the case today.

If you are disabled, you will not be accepted.

Which is a shame.

People must learn to accept everyone.

For if you don't you will not be accepted yourself.

Written by Greg Grant

©2003

MAGIC

Magic is fun.

Magic makes people believe in themselves.

If only we can make magic ourselves.

It will be a lot easier if we can make things disappear.

But we can't

So, we must live with disappointments in our lives.

Till then we must make the most of them.

Written by Greg Grant

©2003

BALL

We are going to have a ball going out with all.

None of us have hit a brick wall.

We are meeting people.

And that's the way it should be.

Singing and dancing.

Having a grand old time.

Leaving our troubles behind.

Getting out to open our minds.

So, tomorrow is not so bad.

Written by Greg Grant
©2003

JOHN

I know a man his name is John.

He is a good man and enjoys a laugh.

He never takes things too seriously.

And he goes with the flow.

When pressure is on, he will show his true colours.

But like Collingwood he will try his best.

But no one beats the mighty tigers.

Written by Greg Grant

©2003

FLOWERS

Flowers are pretty.

Flowers are colourful.

Some have nice scent.

They look good in the garden.

They are good for cuttings and arrangement.

But some don't last forever.

When they die it takes a part of you?

But you must carry on.

Written by Greg Grant

©2003

STREET KID

He lives on the street.

Everyone calls him a freak

If there is a problem, he will see it.

Because he is street smart.

He is the friendliest kid on the block.

But he gets put down.

When people see him, they all laugh at him and call him names.

But one day he did something that made them think.

And then he was treated differently

And now the kid is a street-smart hero.

Written by Greg Grant

©2003

THE BOY WITHIN THE MAN

Every man has got a boy in him.

Just waiting to let him come out and play.

Sometime the boy tries so hard to come out.

But if he comes out, he will get into trouble.

I think not.

He just wants to play.

So, let him.

It's better the boy play instead of the man.

But will the other boys let him play?

Written by Greg Grant

©2003

LOST TOY

I lost my toy.

It was big and fluffy.

I love it dearly.

But I must let go even though I don't want to.

But it's the past.

And sometimes the past is hard to let go.

But to grow up you must let go.

Sometimes the past should be let go.

So, you can head for the future.

Written by Greg Grant

©2003

LET'S FLY

Let's fly far away from here to paradise.

We need to get away.

Somewhere the air is clean.

Away from the noise.

Where we can dream all day long.

And not worry about a thing.

Where we can be free to do what we want.

Let's go to paradise and see what we can find.

Written by Greg Grant

©2003

SHUT DOWN

Please don't shut down on me.

I need you to open and tell me the problem.

Then I can help you.

I know it's hard to open.

But try to.

It will help.

Afterwards you feel well, and life will be clearer.

But if you keep shutting down you will be isolated.

But you don't have to be.

For I am here.

So, open to me.

Written by Greg Grant

©2003

HORSES

Horses are fun to ride.

It's a way to exercise for you and the horse.

With the fresh air going through your hair.

Faster and faster.

Showing off to all.

Then a big jump and of we go over the fence and away on our journey.

Then at the end of the day put him to bed with feed.

Written by Greg Grant

©2003

SCARED

I fear life.

What will become of me tomorrow?

I am not sure whether to live or die.

But being scared brings out the best of me.

We all get scared sometimes.

Being scared sometimes allows us to do things unexpected.

And that could be a good thing.

Life is scary but we must beat it.

And live our lives.

Written by Greg Grant

©2003

PARTY

Let's have a party.

With all the trimmings.

Let's go out with a bang.

We invite all our friends.

With roast pork and a big cake.

Plenty of drink and music.

Let's get smashed.

For we are out to have a good time.

A time to remember.

A time to cheer and be merry.

Written by Greg Grant.

©2003

A TIME TO REMEMBER

Today is a day to remember.

For you have conquered your dreams.

You look back on this day and remember you can do it.

Every day you must be on top.

You must not let things conquer you.

Every day you must at least conquer one thing.

When you conquer everything, you can move on to bigger thing.

And it will be a time to remember.

Written by Greg Grant

©2003

LOVE

Love is a wonderful feeling.

It is necessary for life.

Love between man and a woman is happy and peaceful time.

Love lasts for a lifetime.

It brings meaning to the whole life.

When you find love, you will know it.

You will feel happy and calm in yourself.

It is like a whole new light in your life.

It gives you some joy.

Written by Greg Grant

©2003

NOT A DAY GOES BY

There is not a day goes by that I don't think of you.

The good time and the bad.

You will always be in my heart.

Our friendship did mean a lot to me.

You let me cry on your shoulder.

And we have seen it all through.

I know we must part.

One day we will meet again.

Till then goodbye my dear friend.

Written by Greg Grant

©2003

STREET

My street is not my own anymore.

It has changed from good to bad.

I have seen it all.

Makes me wonder if it is time to go.

But where should I go?

It's been a long time.

But things change.

Sometime for the good.

But not for me

Written by Greg Grant

©2003

GOOD THING

We have a good thing going.

Please don't stop.

It feels so right.

If you change it, you may not get it back.

So, leave it and keep on playing.

If you change it now you might get people offside.

And you don't want that.

Written by Greg Grant

©2003

SPEED

Everything is done with speed.

Faster and faster we go.

Until we run down.

Then we need time out to recharge

Then on our way we go again.

Starting all over again.

The cycle never ends.

Written by Greg Grant
©2003

CRY

We all cry sometimes.

Some people cry for other people.

Some people cry instead of getting angry.

We all cry when we get hurt.

Some people even cry when they are happy.

Even when they have lost a loved one.

People even cry them selves to sleep at night.

Or cry for help.

So, when you see someone crying.

Ask them what's wrong for they may need your help.

And you never know you may win a friend.

Written by Greg Grant

©2003

CORNER

I am stuck in a corner.

Trying to get out.

But every time I do someone puts me right back angry.

People don't want me to get hurt.

But one thing they don't realize they are making me angry.

It they don't let me get up from the corner I will never grow up.

Written by Greg Grant

©2003

STORM

There is a storm brewing out there.

A ship stuck in it.

What shall we do?

Shall we save it?

We can't let the people drown.

If we save them, they will thank us.

And we will be heroes.

Written by Greg Grant

©2003

LET PRAY

Prayers are made to be heard.

Prayers are helpful.

When we have troubles, we go and pray.

Pray to be heard.

Pray for everything.

Pray for your friends, family and animals.

Pray for a sick person.

Pray for healthy people.

Pray for loved ones.

Also pray for yourself.

Pray to be good at something.

Every time you pray, you're heard by God.

And he will hear you.

So, lets pray for our own health.

Pray everyday; find a quiet spot to do it in.

Prayer works.

Written by Greg Grant
©2003

THE INVISIBLE MAN

There's this man who is capable of being invisible.

Fighting crime with ease.

Being invisible when ever he wants to.

To him it is a gift.

He can get away from it all.

When things get too much for him.

He just turns on the invisible ray.

It you see something falling it must be the invisible man.

He can help police with catching crooks.

Because he is the invisible man.

Written by Greg Grant

©2003

FRIENDS

Friends are a must to have.

Friends are to talk to.

You can go with them and have fun.

Even have a drink with them and have fun.

Or a laugh.

Talk about the issues of today.

But don't make them mad because you might lose them.

If you find the right friend, they can be good for you.

Written by Greg Grant

©2003

WILIAM THE GREAT

There is a young man they call William.

He is a great young man.

He can do many a wonderful thing.

He is a person who you can look up to.

For one day he will be king.

He has a cheerful face and is warm hearted.

Everyone enjoys his company.

He can make people laugh.

When he reaches 21, he will be bigger than Ben Hur.

He will get lots of presents.

But the biggest present of all is people's love and respect.

So have a happy birthday for our prince.

Written by Greg Grant

©2003

THE LADY IN RED

I saw her out of the corner of my eye.

She was just standing their beautiful flowing hair and in a bright red dress.

I strolled over and asked her if she wanted to

dance. She accepted with a big smile.

So, we danced the night away.

When we finished, I took her over to the bar and brought her a drink.

And we talked and talked.

At the end of the night I asked her out one night.

She was the nicest woman three.

So, we went out later that week.

It was a nice night.

And I am seeing her again.

Written by Greg Grant

©2003

BRAVE HEART

We all must be brave sometimes.

Even if we don't show it.

Even the scariest things we must be brave for.

Being brave is a good thing to be.

Bravery can help you get through life.

Brave people are good people.

Bravery is walking down the street with people staring at you.

Bravery is taking the good with the bad.

Written by Greg Grant

©2003

FLASH LIGHTING

His name is Sebastian.

With a white coat and mane.

He looks very smart and gentle.

He will take you on his back

He will take orders from you.

He won't buck or bite.

Just listen to you.

He runs like flash lighting.

And jumps very high.

He's the kindest and gentlest horse in the playground.

His name is Sebastian.

Written by Greg Grant
©2003

GO TO THE PEOPLE

Today is a happy day for one and all.

Today a baby is born.

His name is Luke.

A beautiful bundle of joy.

So, tell one and all.

One day he will be a great person.

For he can heal people.

He can stop the fighting.

He can change history.

So, everyone shouts for joy.

Written by Greg Grant

©2003

I AM LOST

I am lost and don't know where to turn.

All my friends have deserted me.

I believe so much in people, but they don't believe in me.

Where did they all go?

I want them back.

They're all scared of me.

One day I will win them back.

Written by Greg Grant

©2003

PAIN

The pain is unbearable.

When will is stop?

A good life turned upside down and inside out.

But you still must live.

Everyday is harder than the next.

So, now you're living one day at a time.

All those dreams you have had are put on hold.

But one day something will happen for the good.

Written by Greg Grant

©2003

VOICES IN MY HEAD

There are voices in my head.

They are not letting me sleep.

They are making me insane.

I have been down that path a long time ago.

I don't want them to return.

But slowly they are.

They will make sure they drag me down.

It could be my imagination.

But it can't be.

They sound so real.

Written by Greg Grant
©2003

SO, IT'S REAL

It's unmistakable it can't be real.

It feels fake.

Can it be true?

For no one believes you only me.

What does it take for people to believe you?

If it is true how come no one told me.

We won't really know.

Years from now it will come out.

By then it will be too late.

Written by Greg Grant

©2003

SWEET MUSIC

I listen to sweet music.

It calms me down and makes me relax.

So, I can sleep with ease.

It is good for the soul and the mind.

Some music has good rhythm.

It makes you so relaxed you can think clearer.

It makes you think of things to write.

You can also sing to music.

Sweet music is the way to go

Written by Greg Grant

©2003

WALKING IN THE FOREST

Let's go for a walk in the forest.

We won't get lost for we have God on our side.

He will make sure the sun is shining on us.

He will show us the way forward.

He will keep the devil at bay.

So, let's take a walk on the road of everlasting life.

Take a walk with me.

Written by Greg Grant

©2003

HEAVEN

There is a place they call paradise.

It is a nice place where there is no fighting or anger.

We will all be there one day.

When you get there, your soul will be saved.

It is a happy place filled with music and angels that will look after you.

But you must be good to get there.

It is a place where we have everlasting life.

So be good and you will be rewarded.

Written by Greg Grant

©2003

PLEASE COME HOME

I don't know what I did wrong.

I am sure I can sort out the problem.

If you only come home, we can talk about it.

So, baby won't you please come home.

I miss you and I find it hard without you here.

I am sure it is not a big deal.

If we can only talk it out.

So, baby please come home.

Written by Greg Grant

©2003